# Animals Portrait & Mandalas
## Coloring Boook for Adults

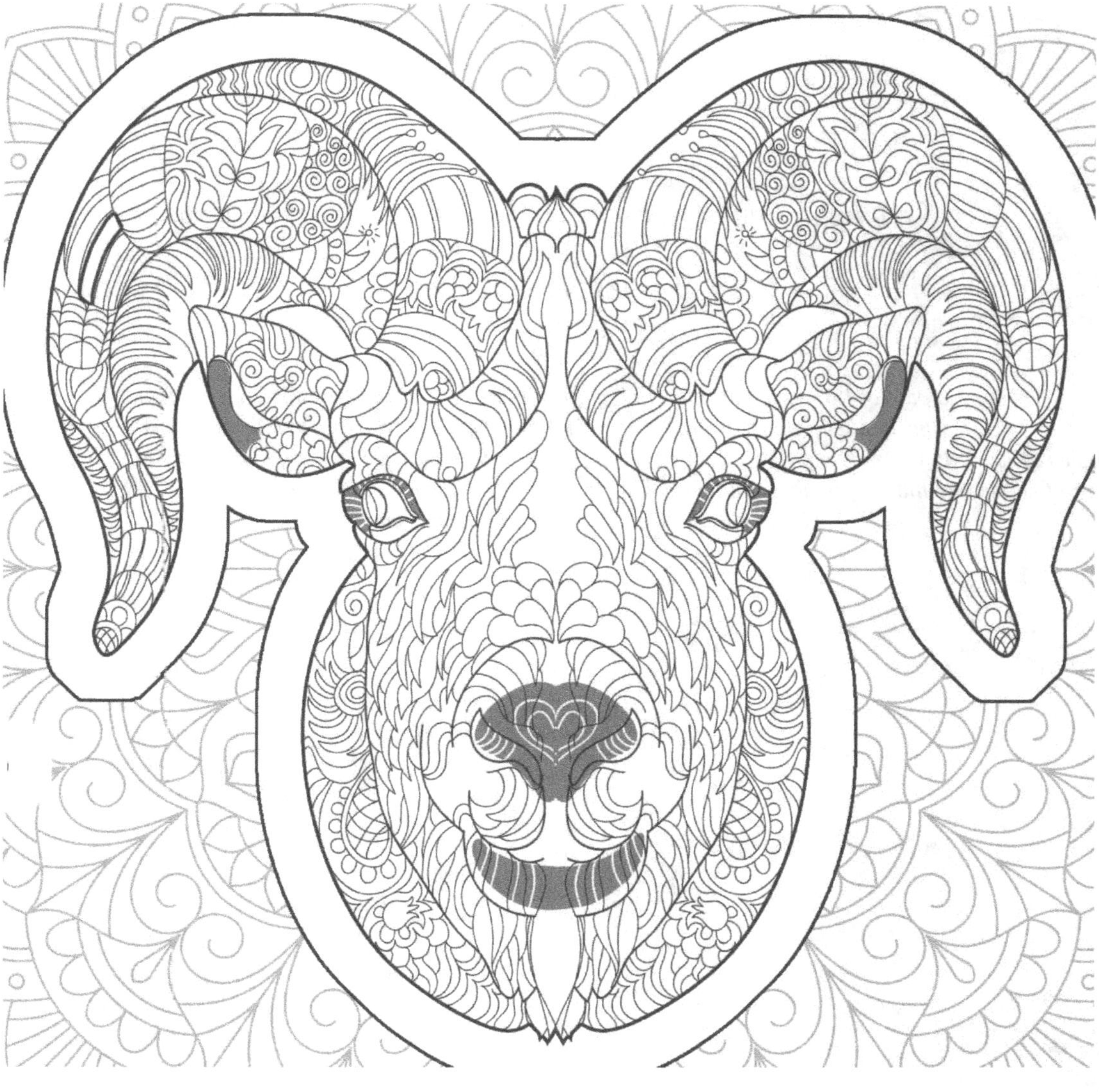

*Sophia Payne*

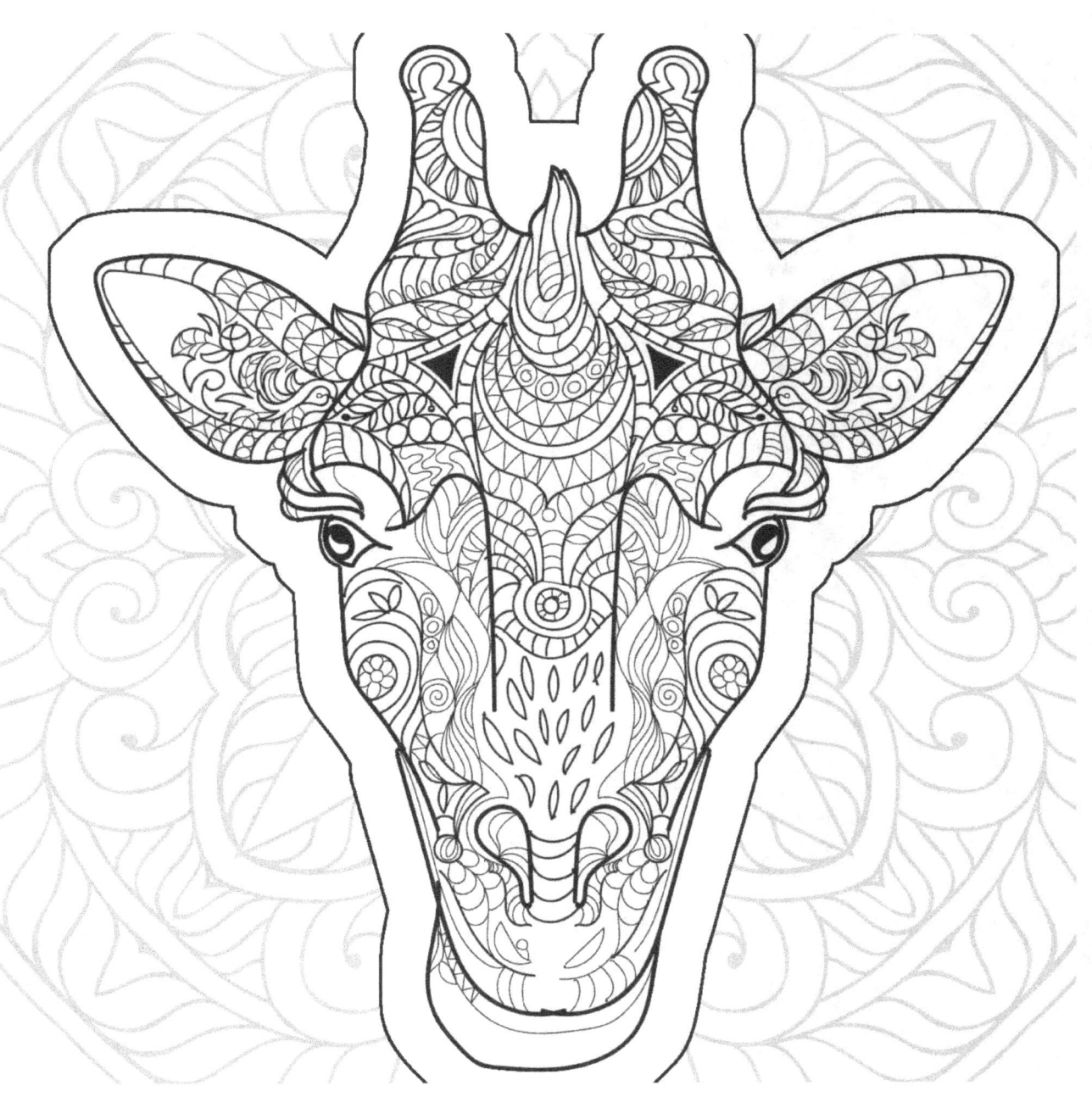

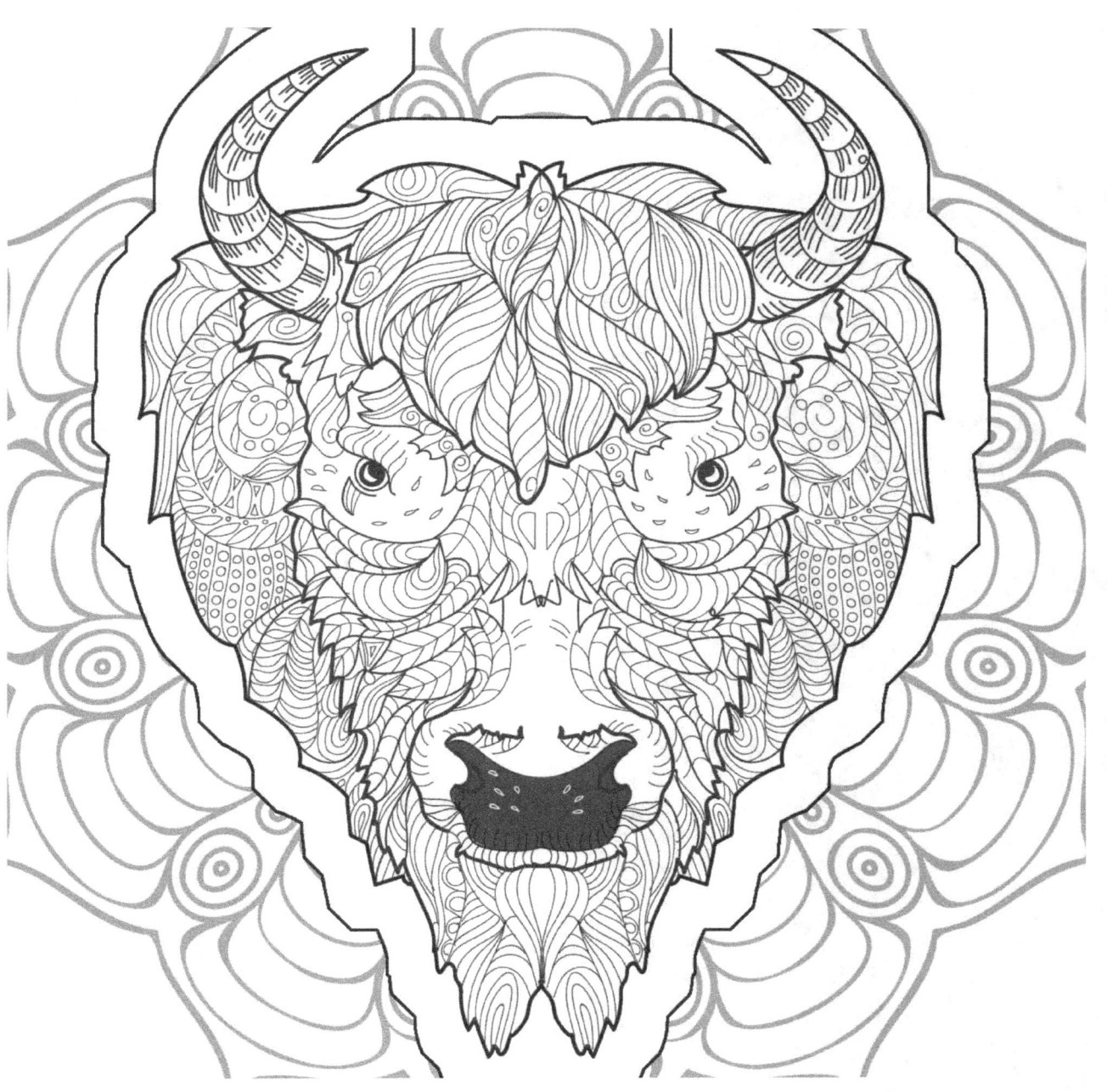

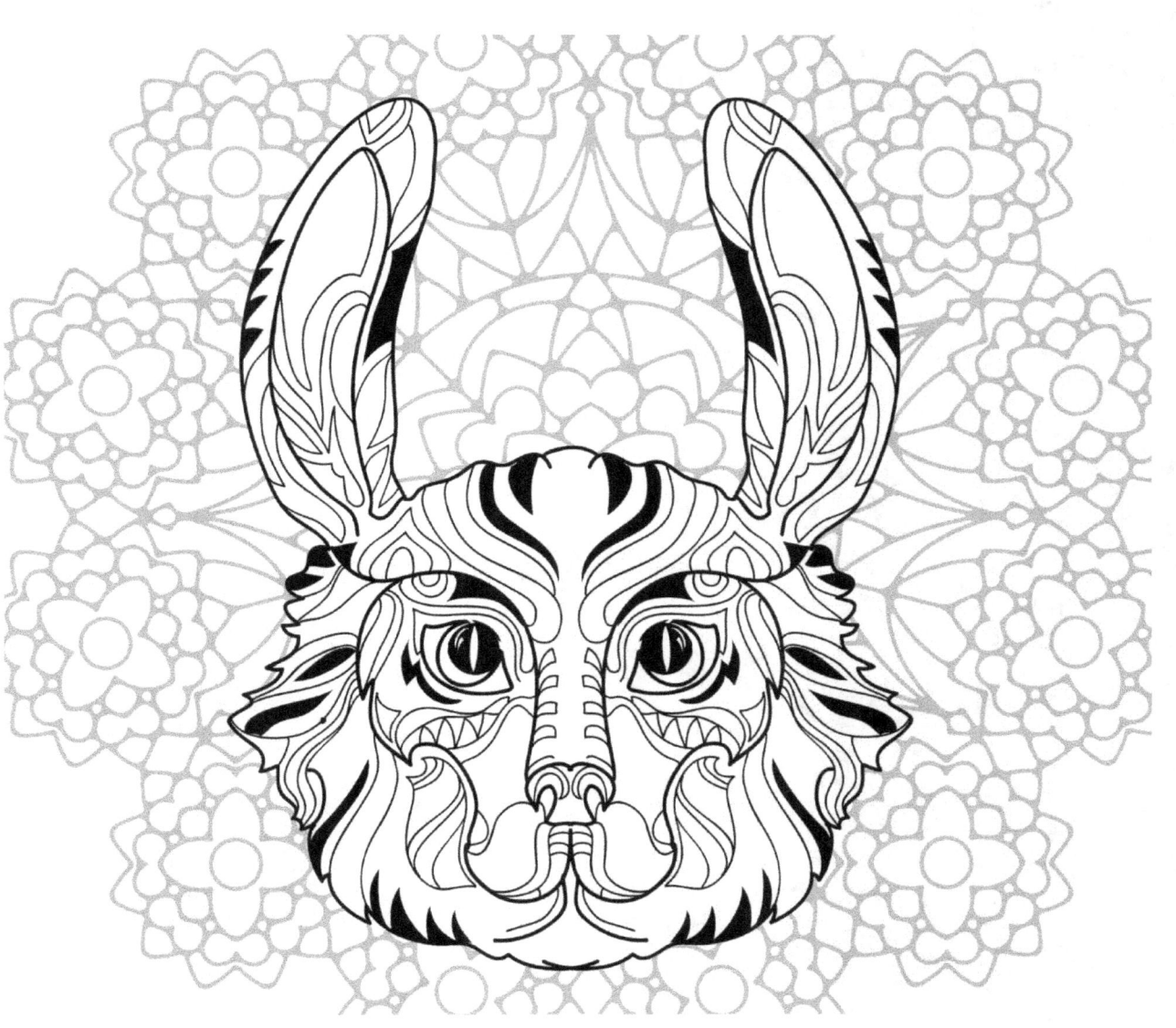

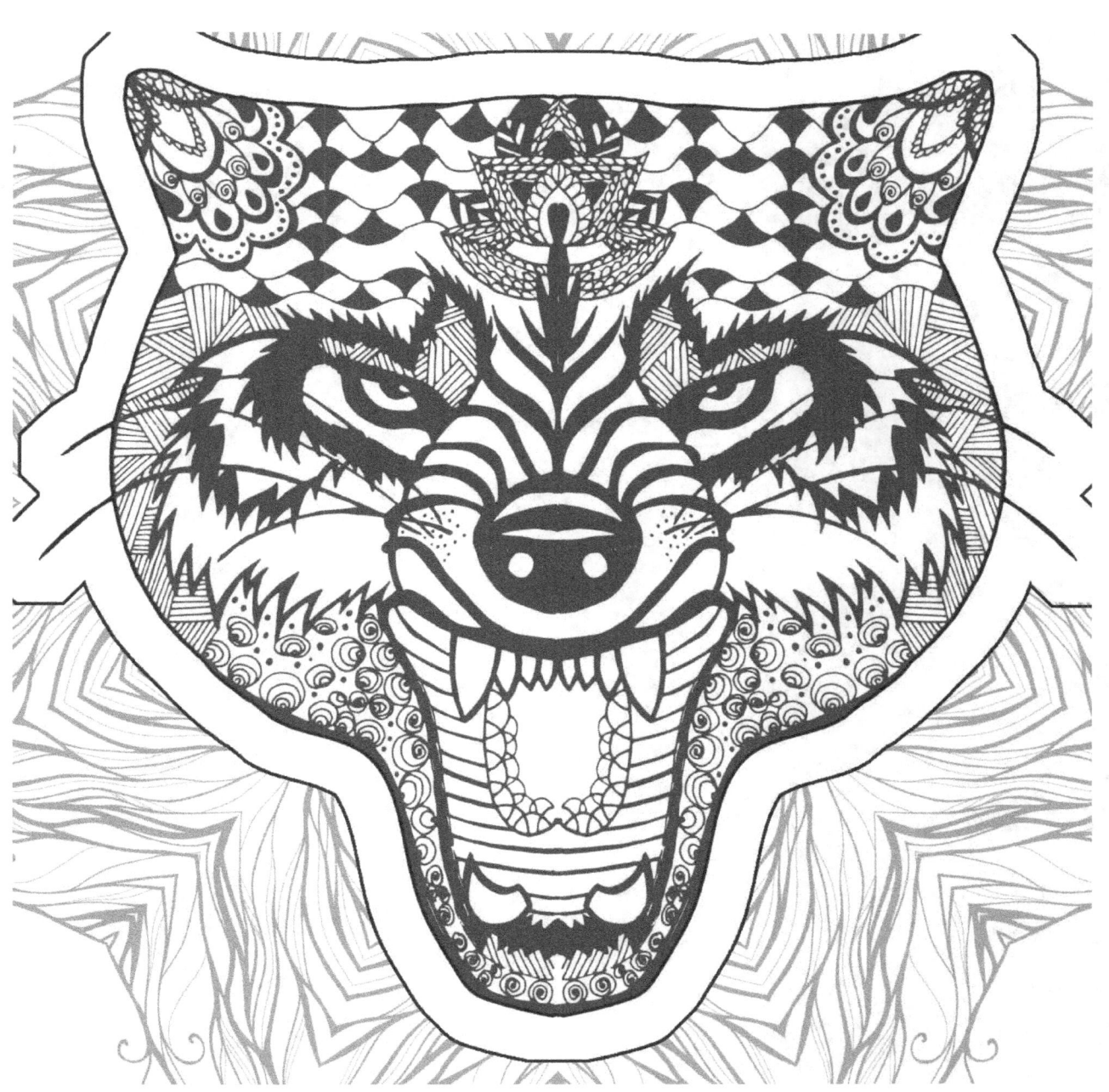

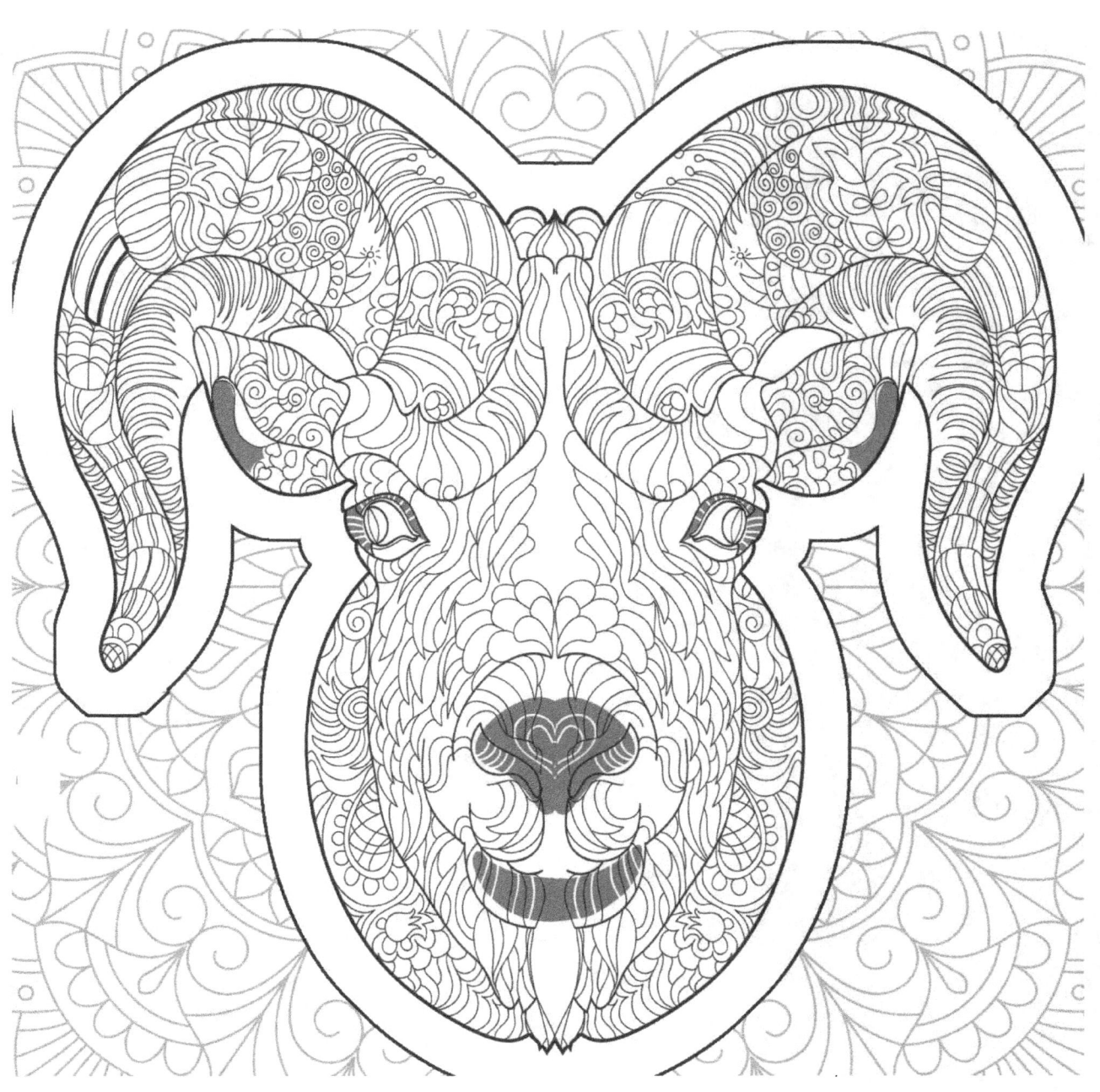

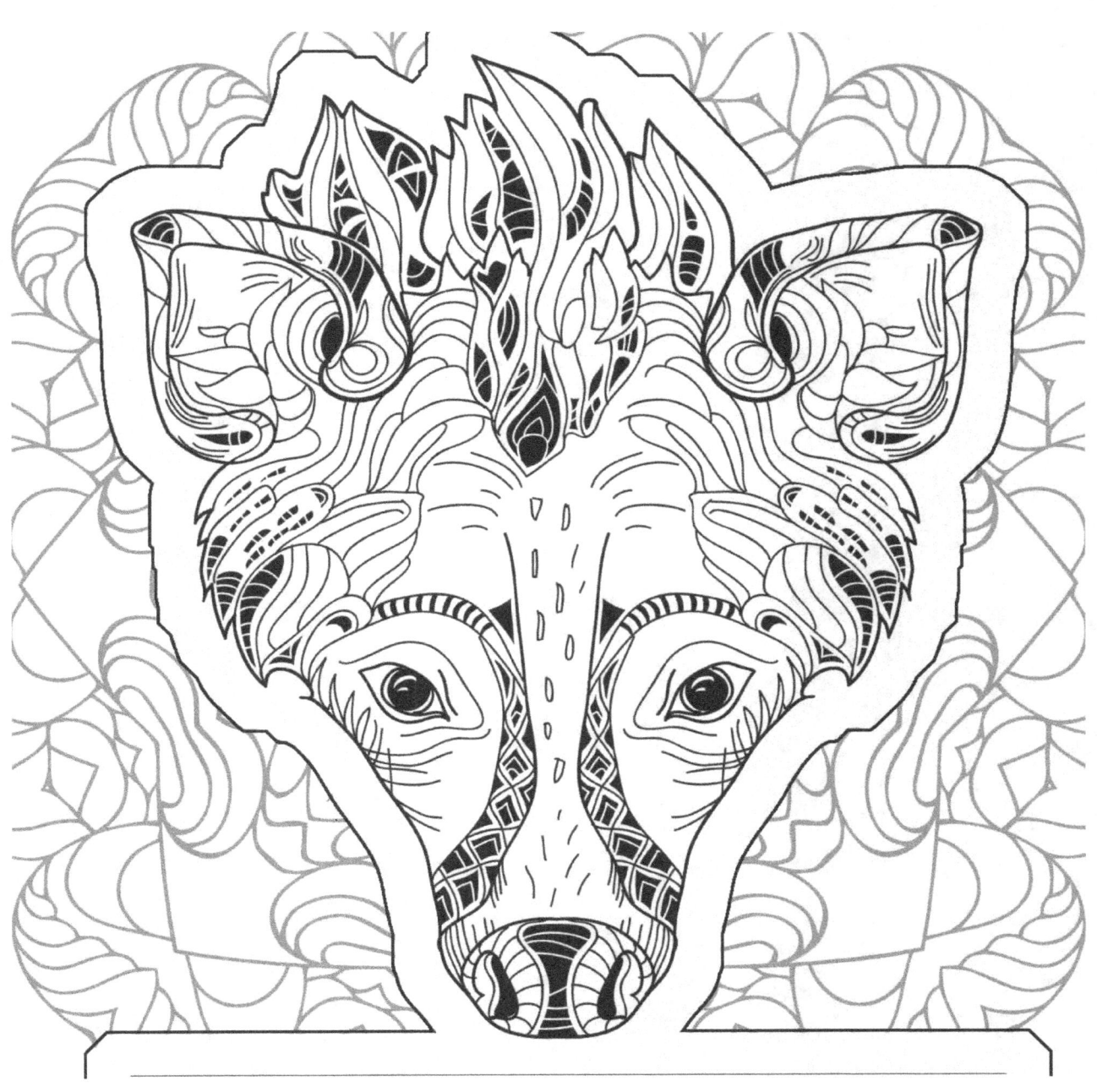

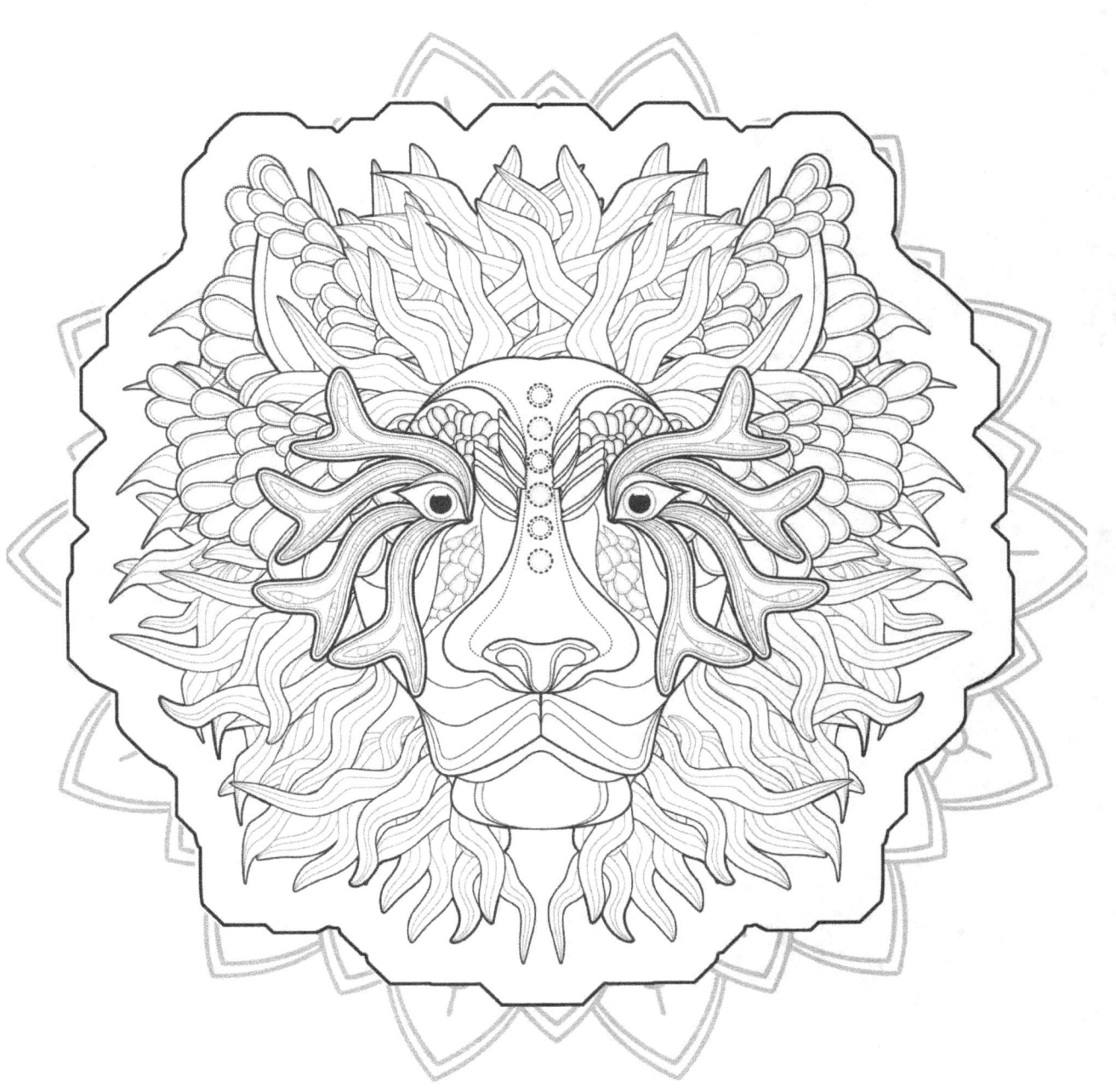

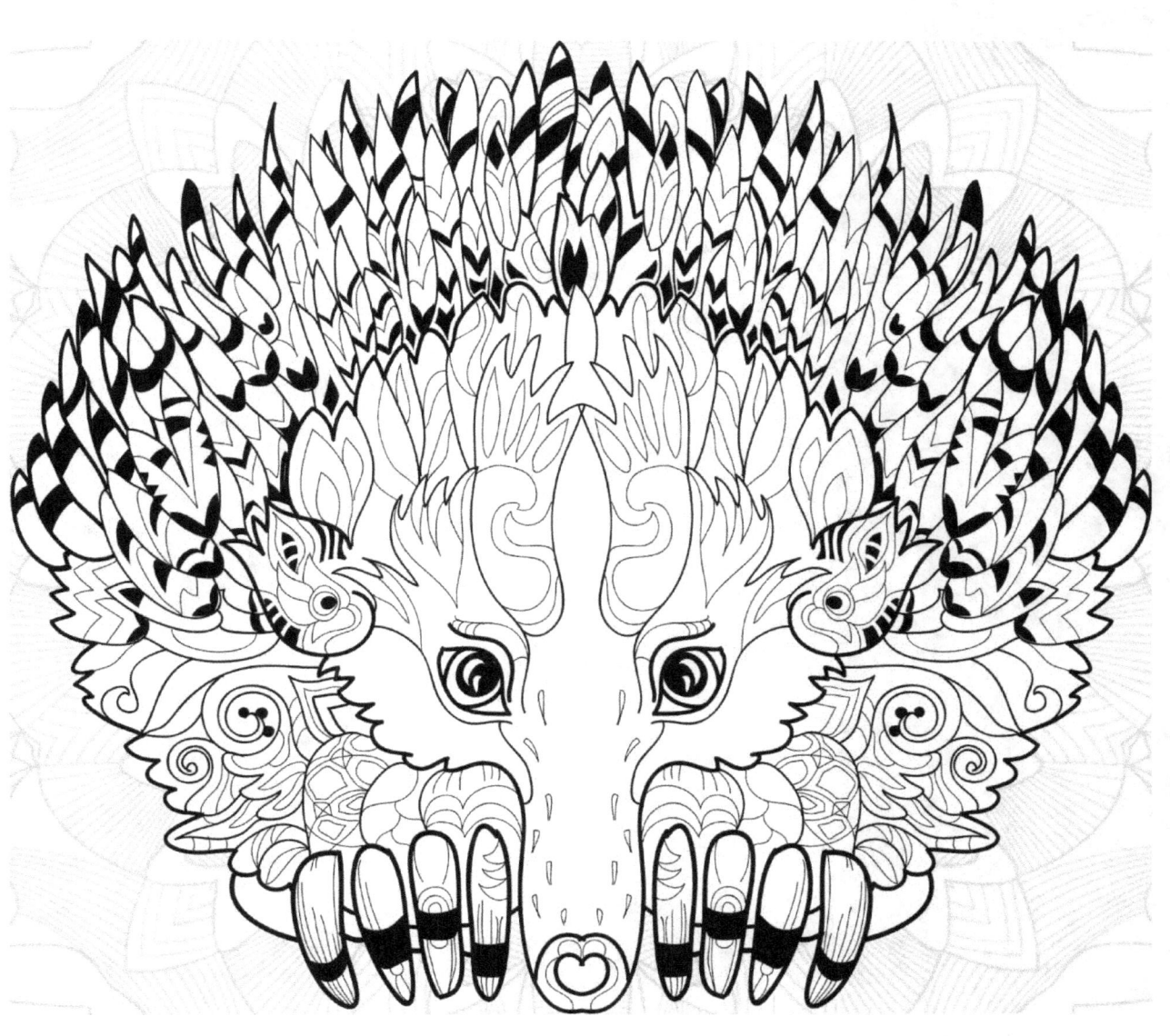

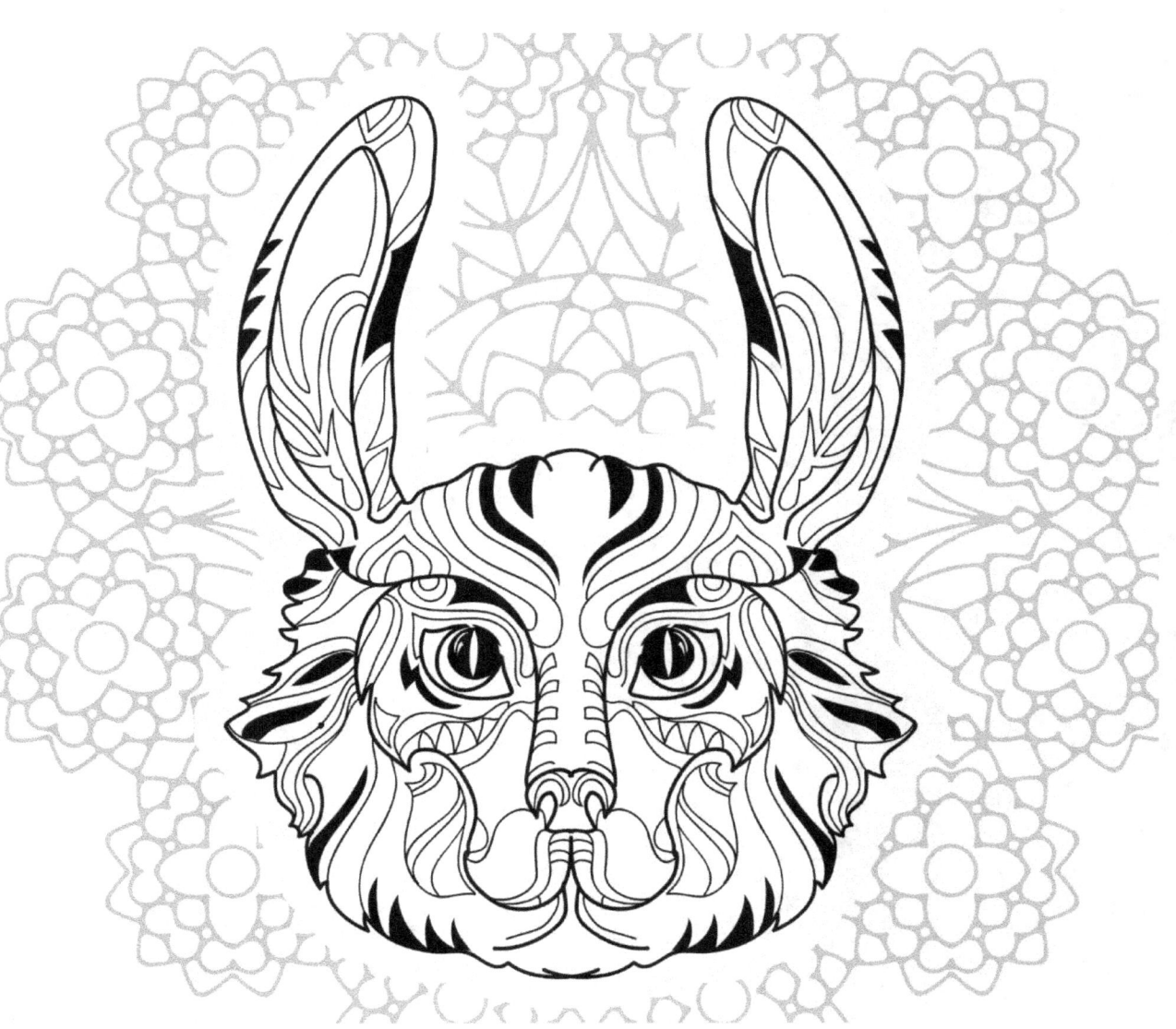

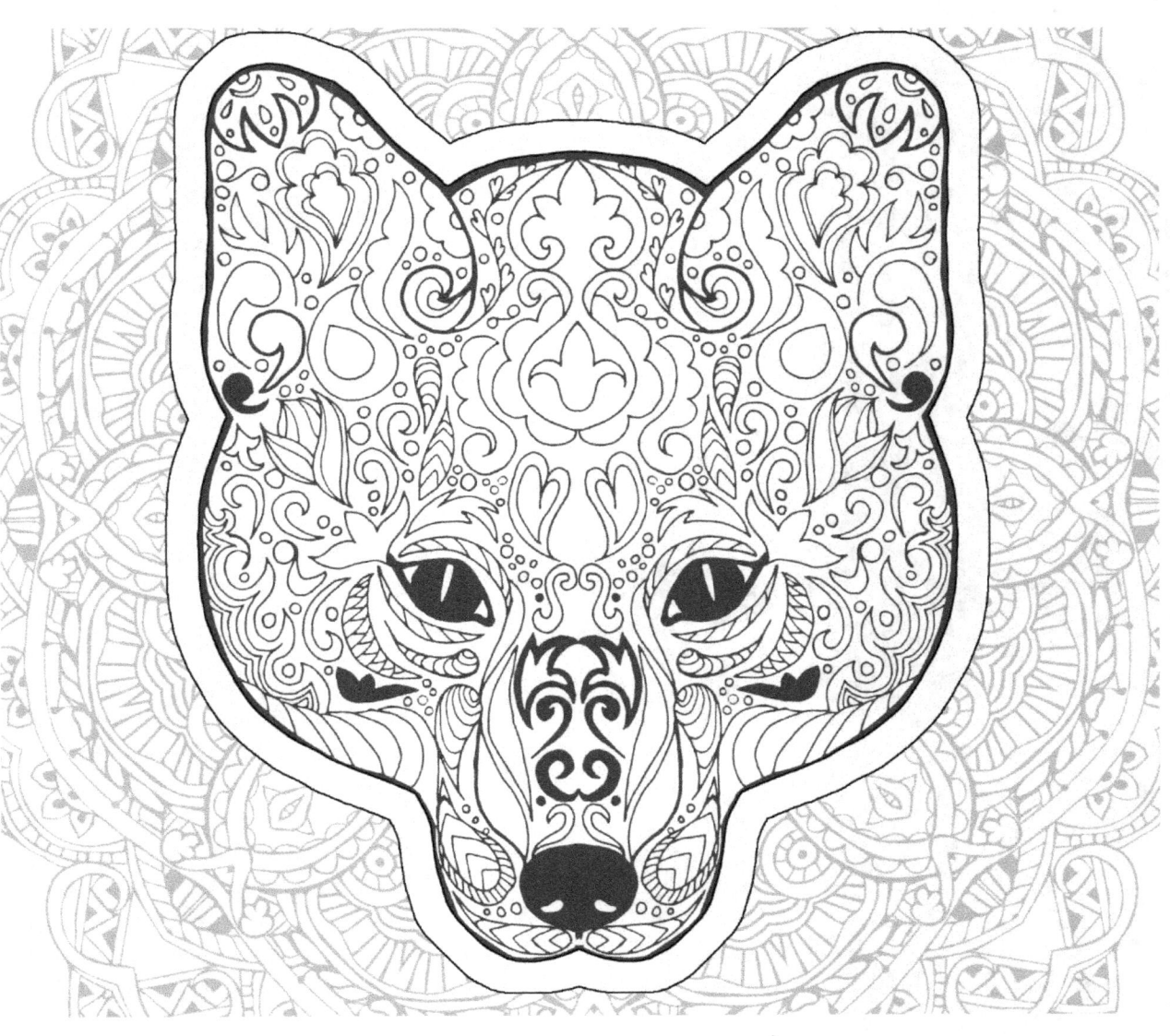

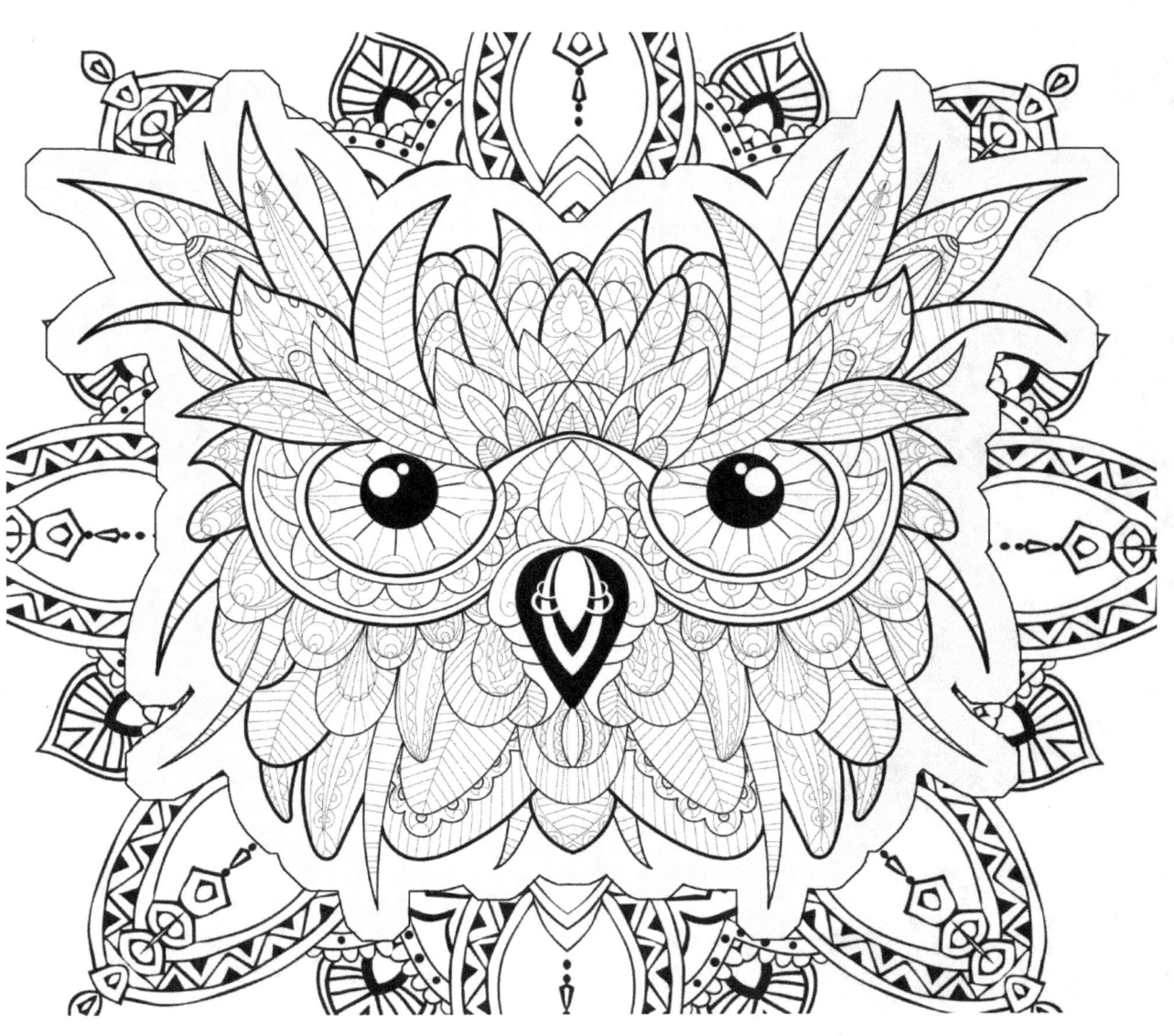

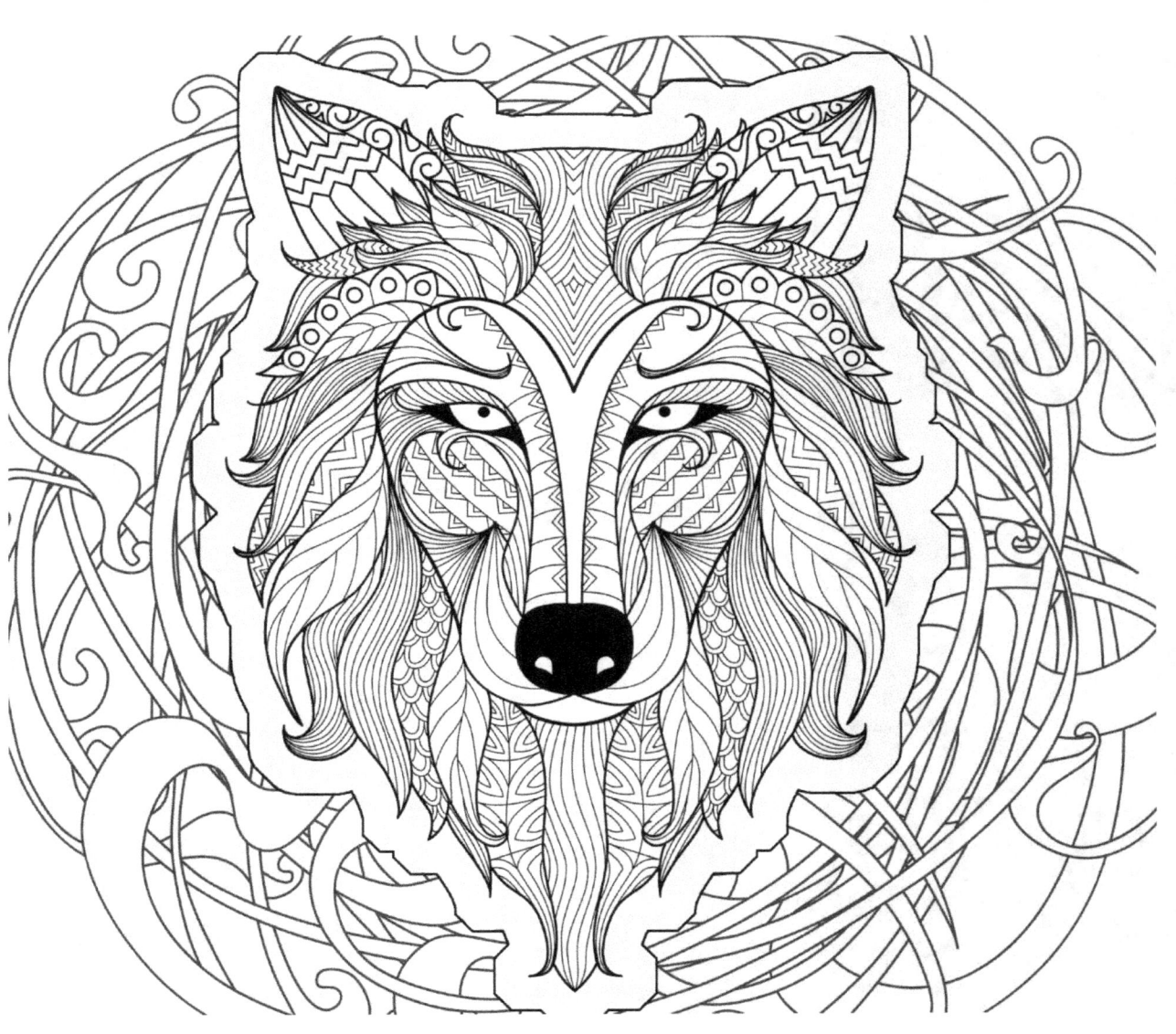

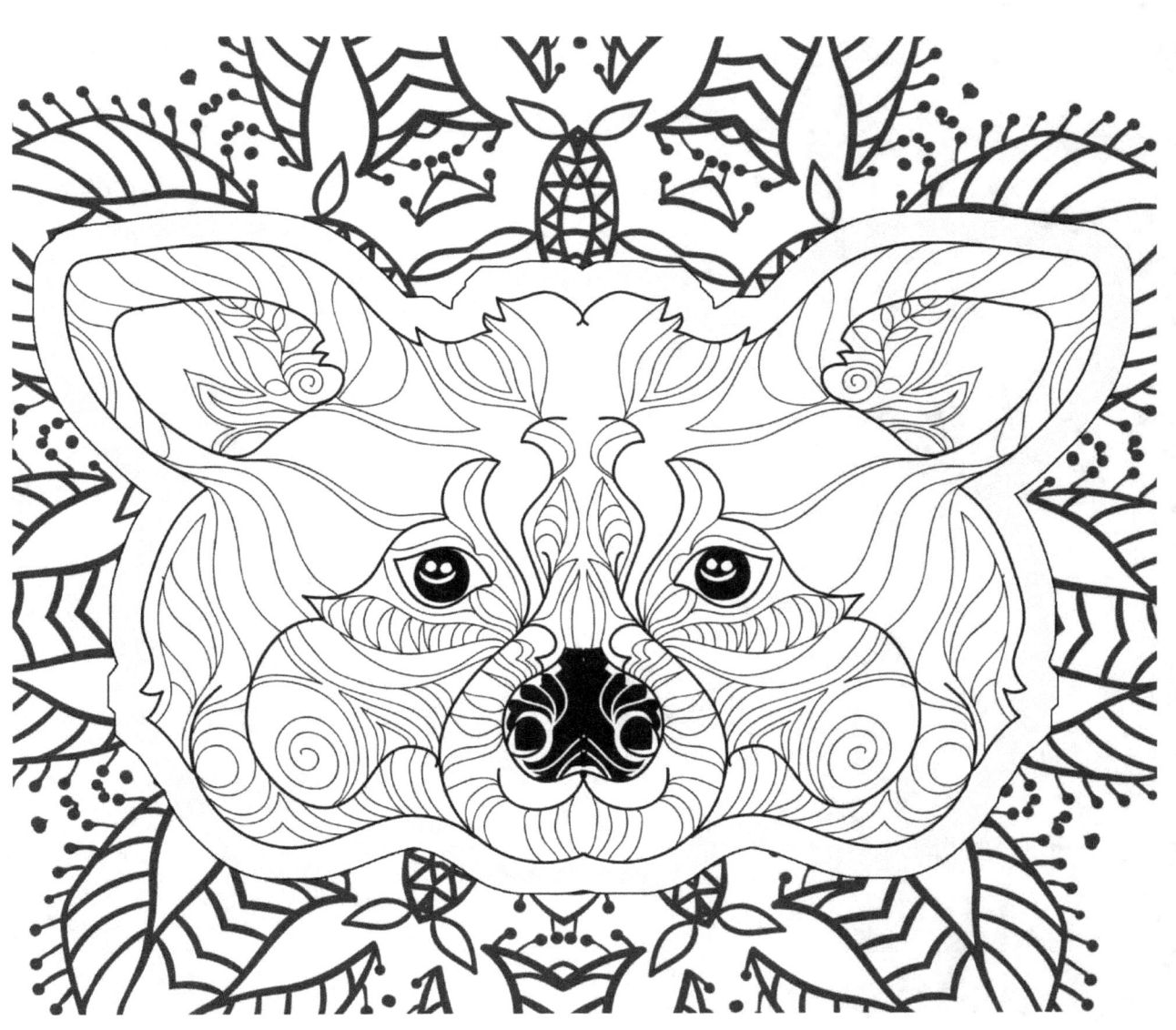

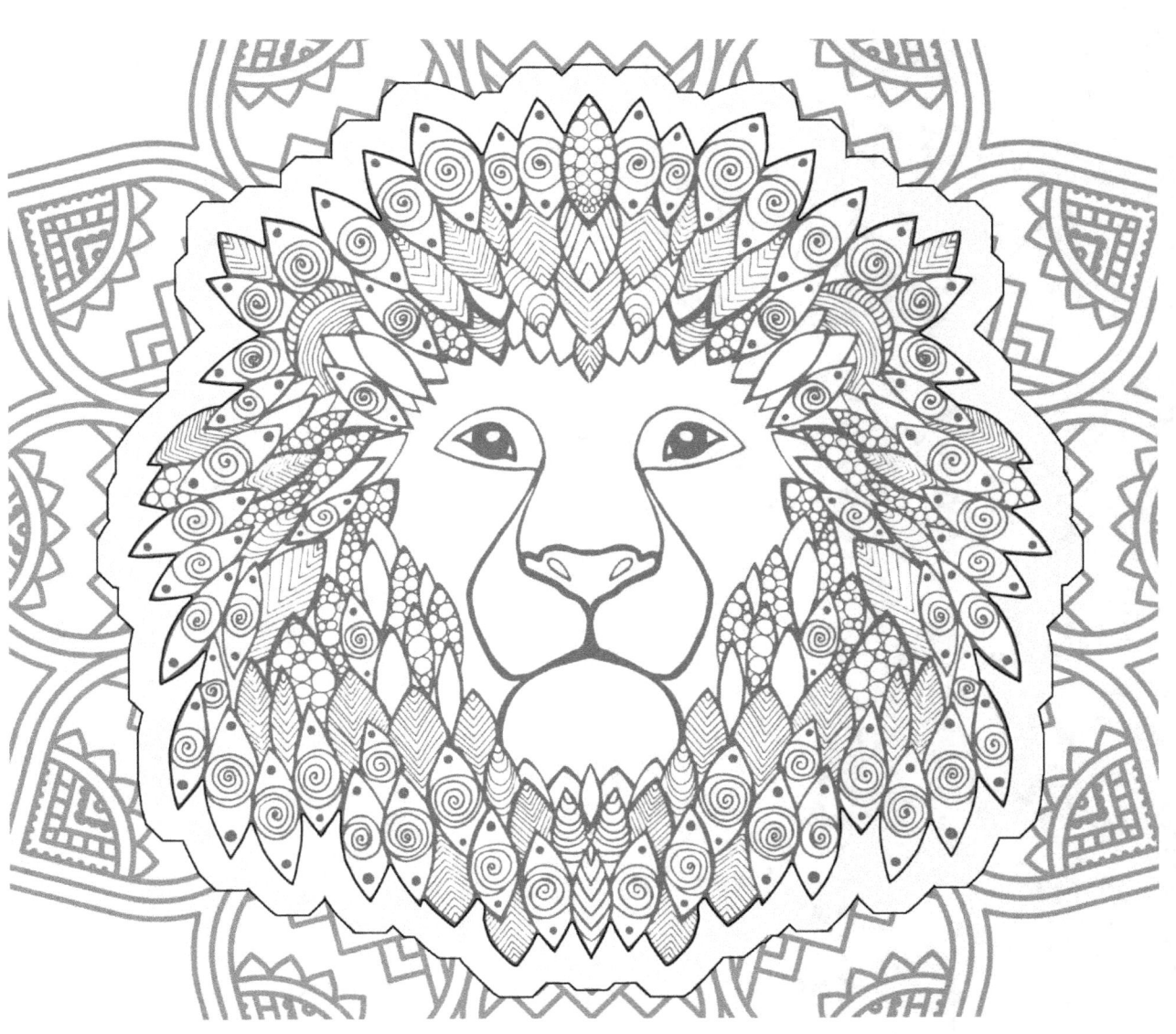

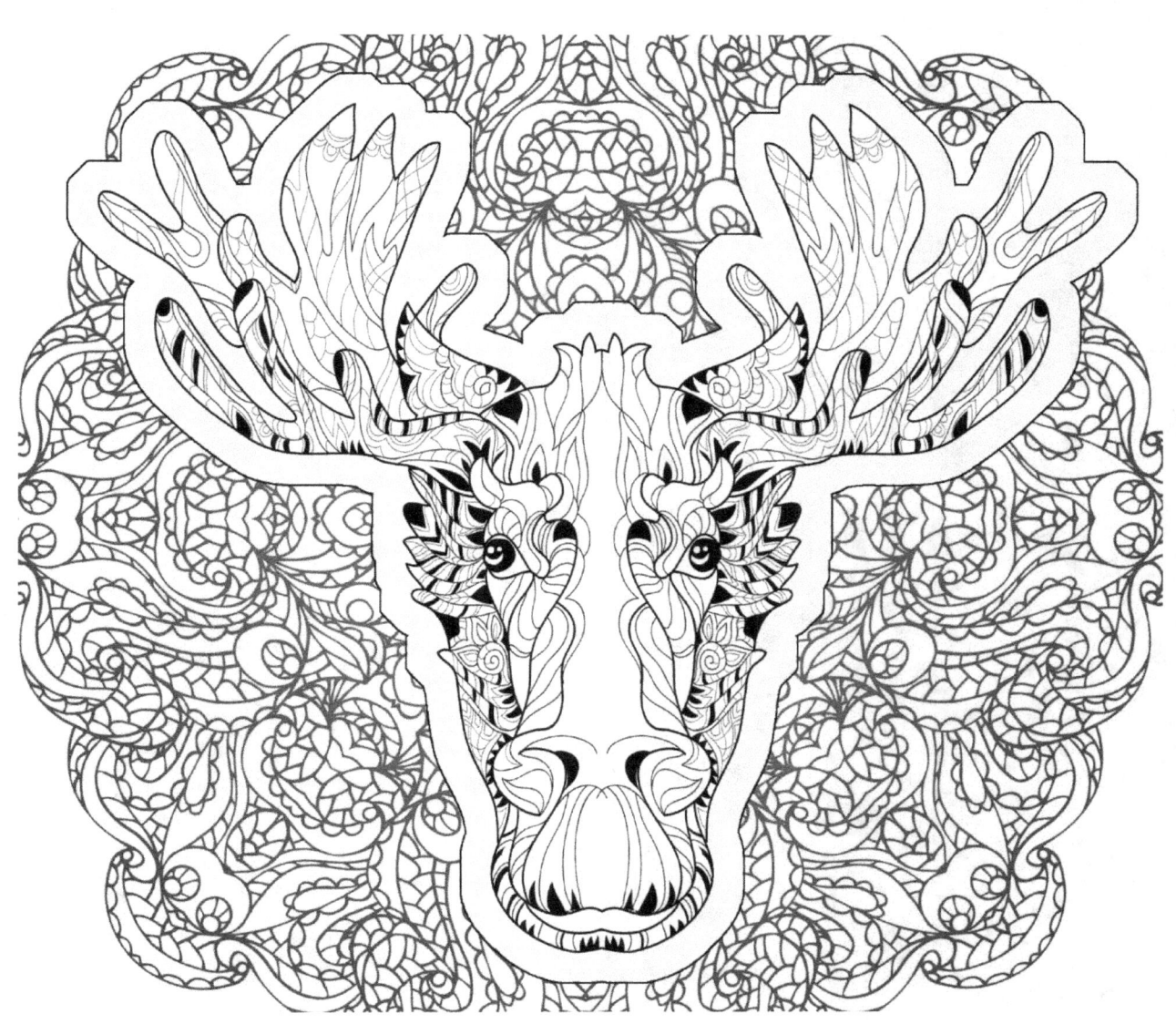

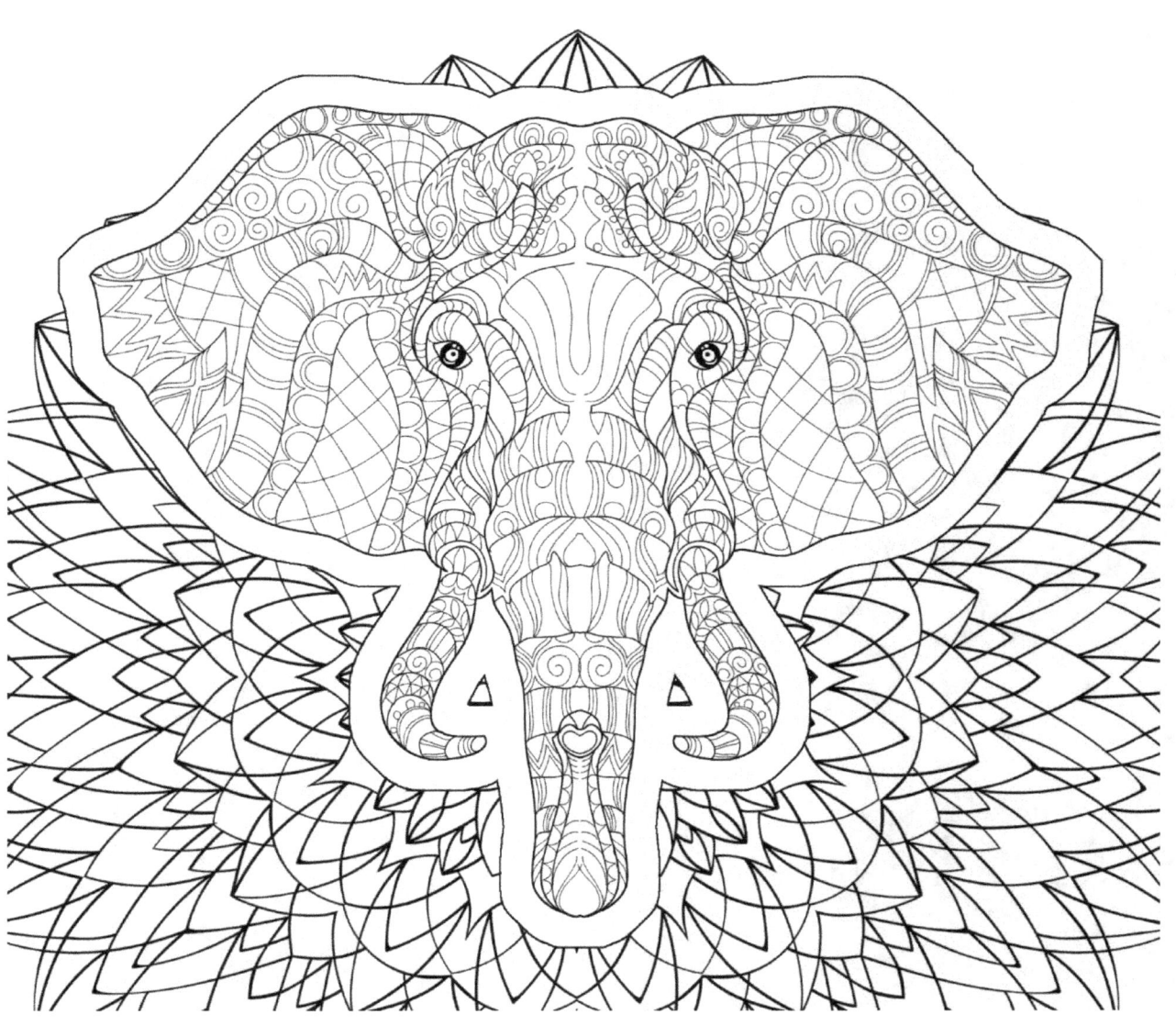

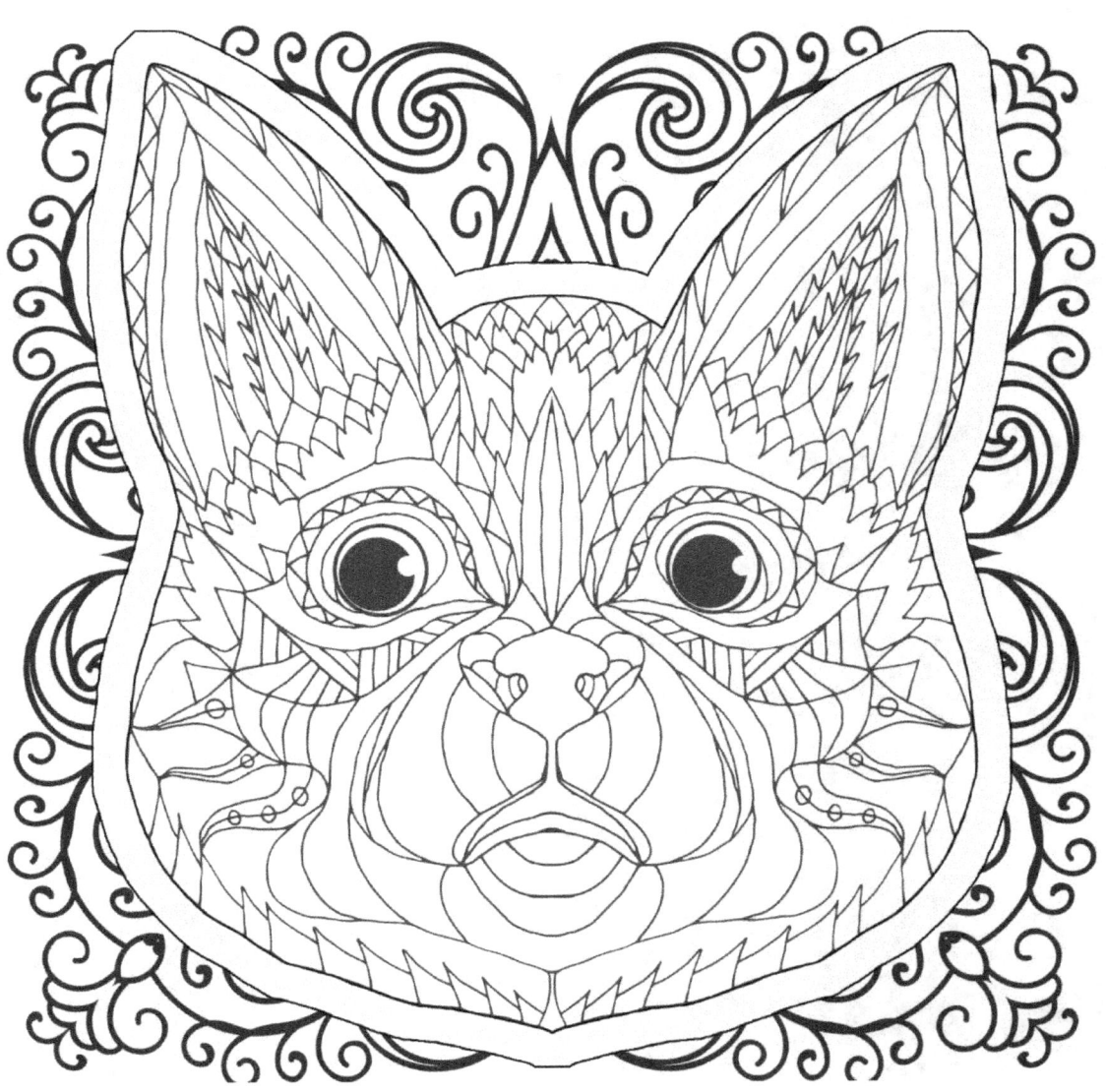

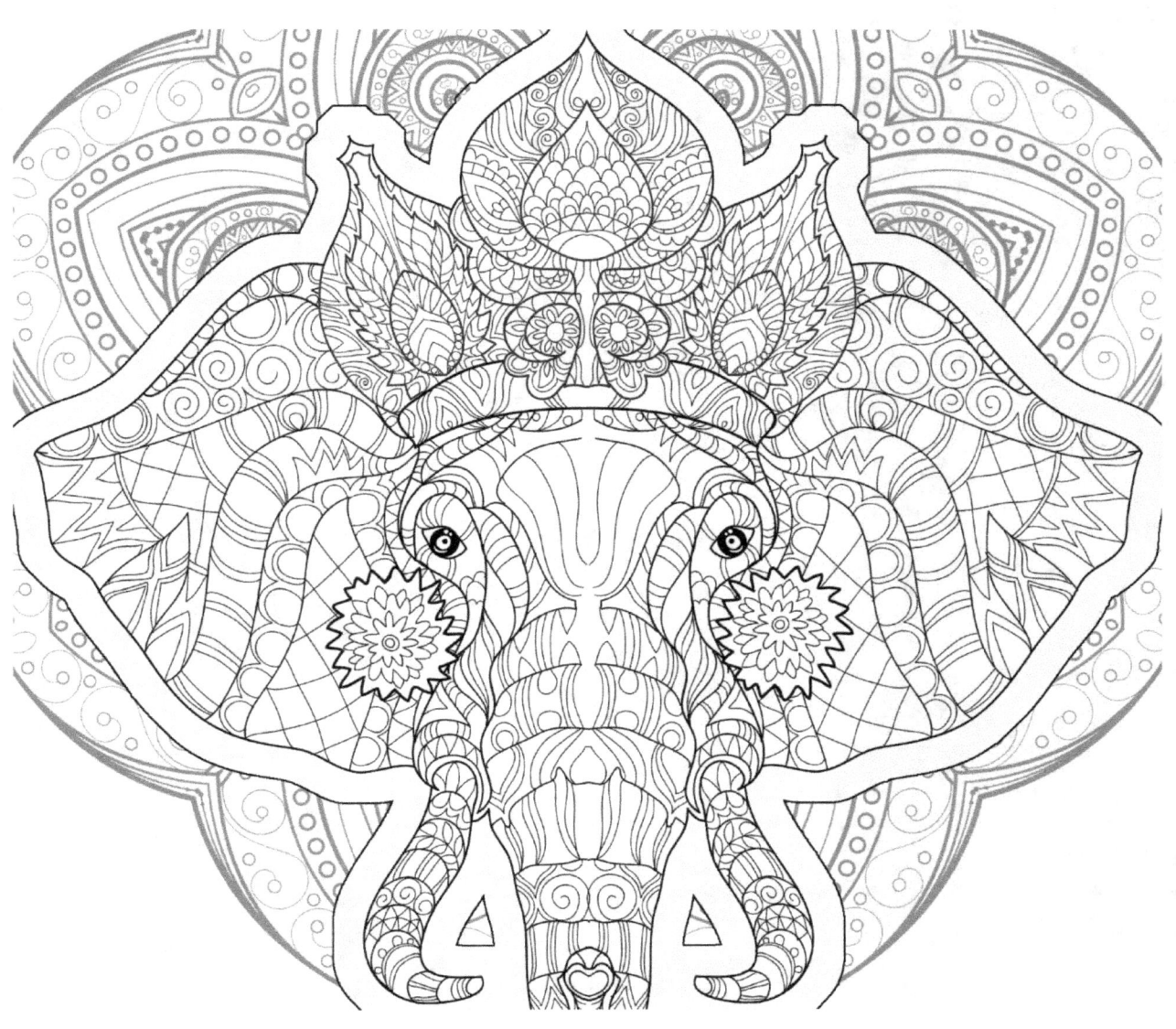

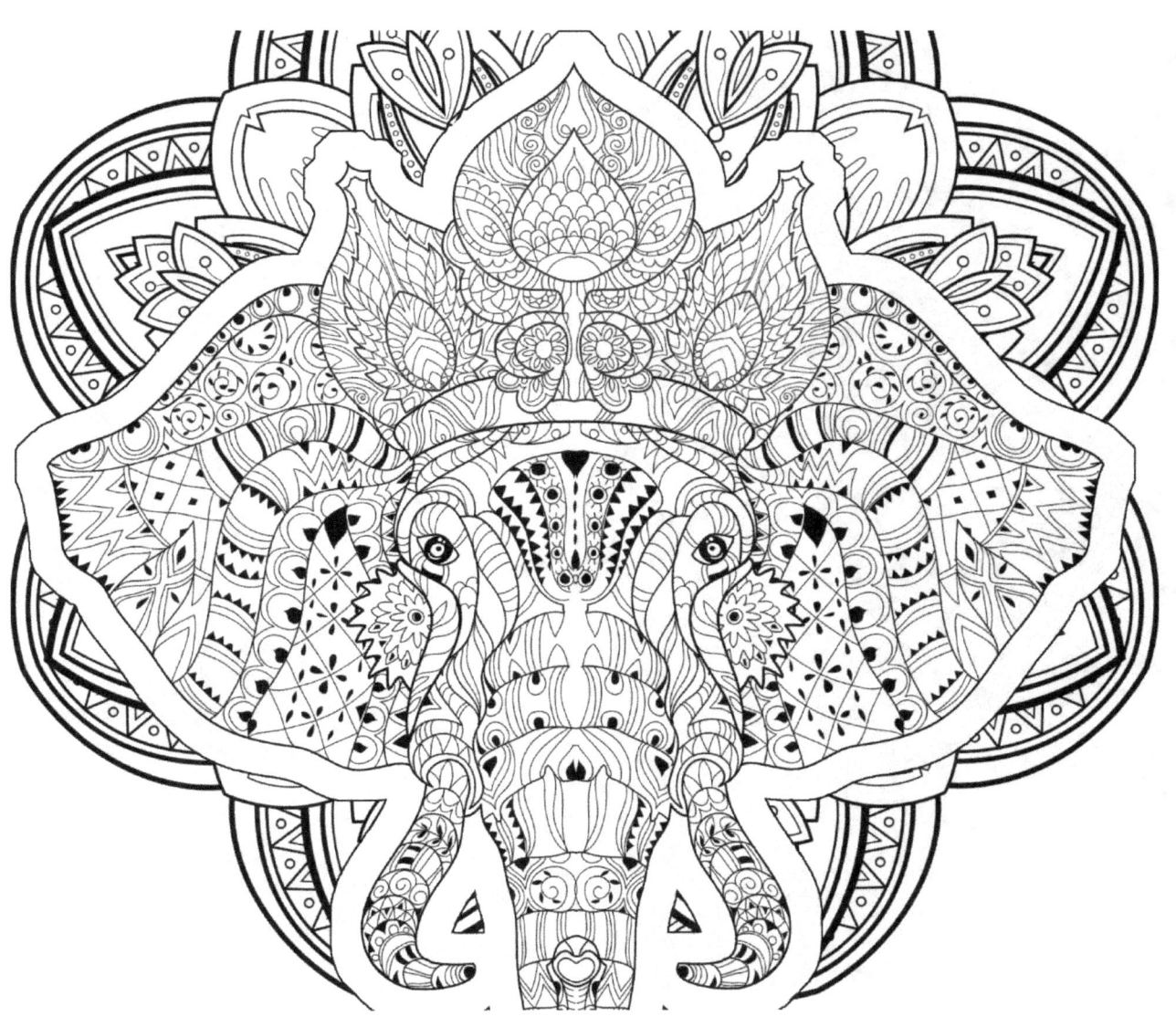

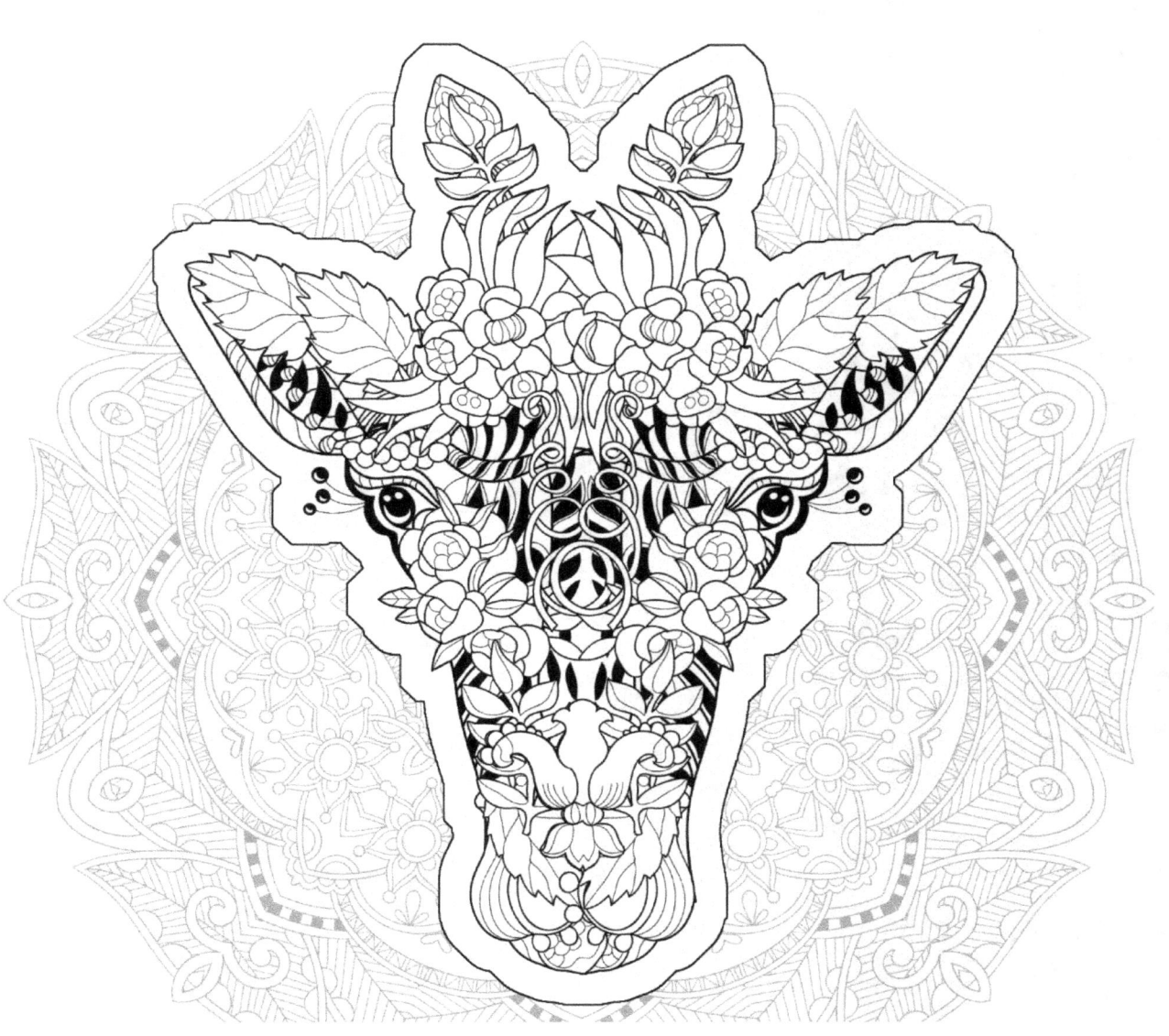

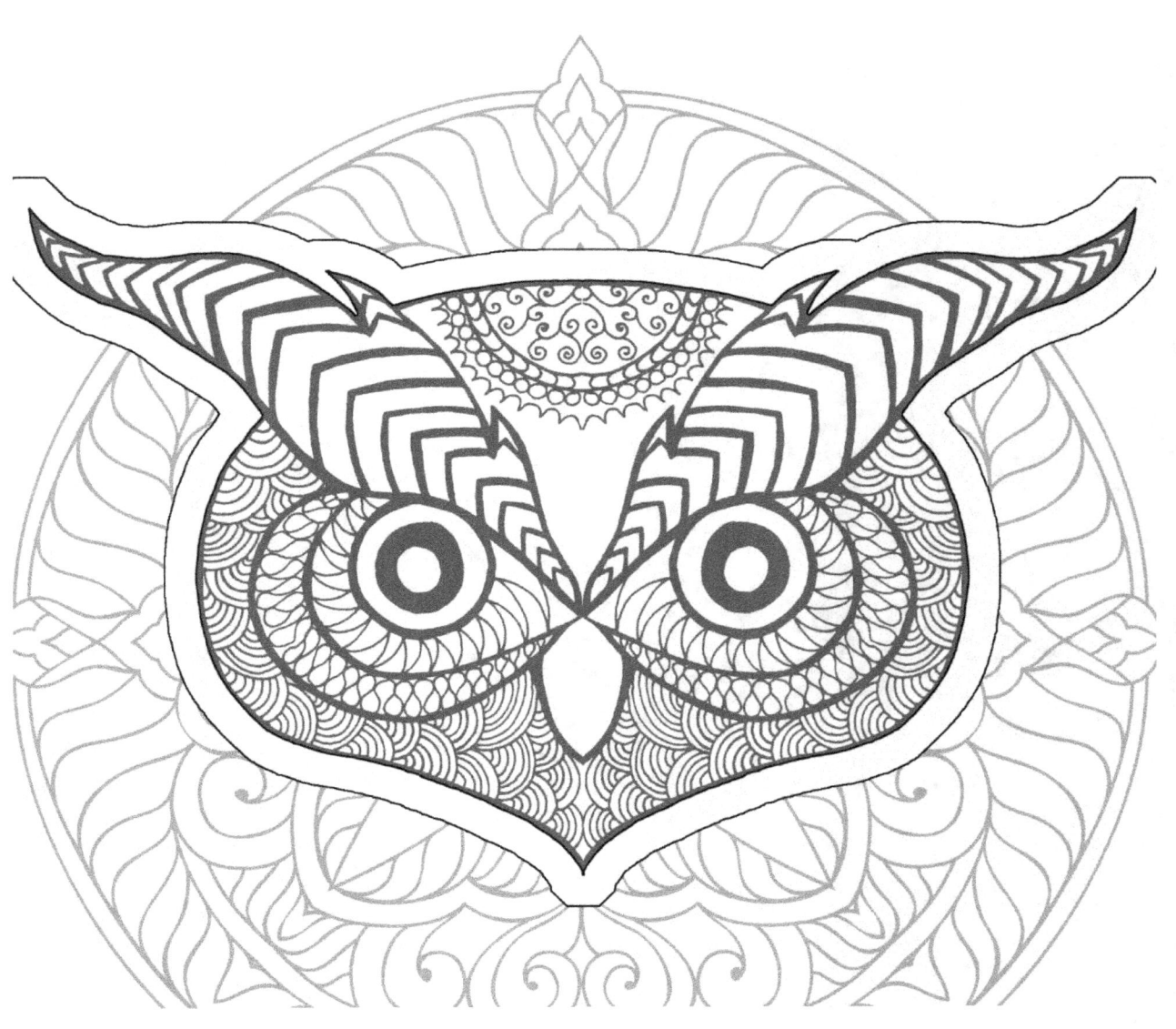

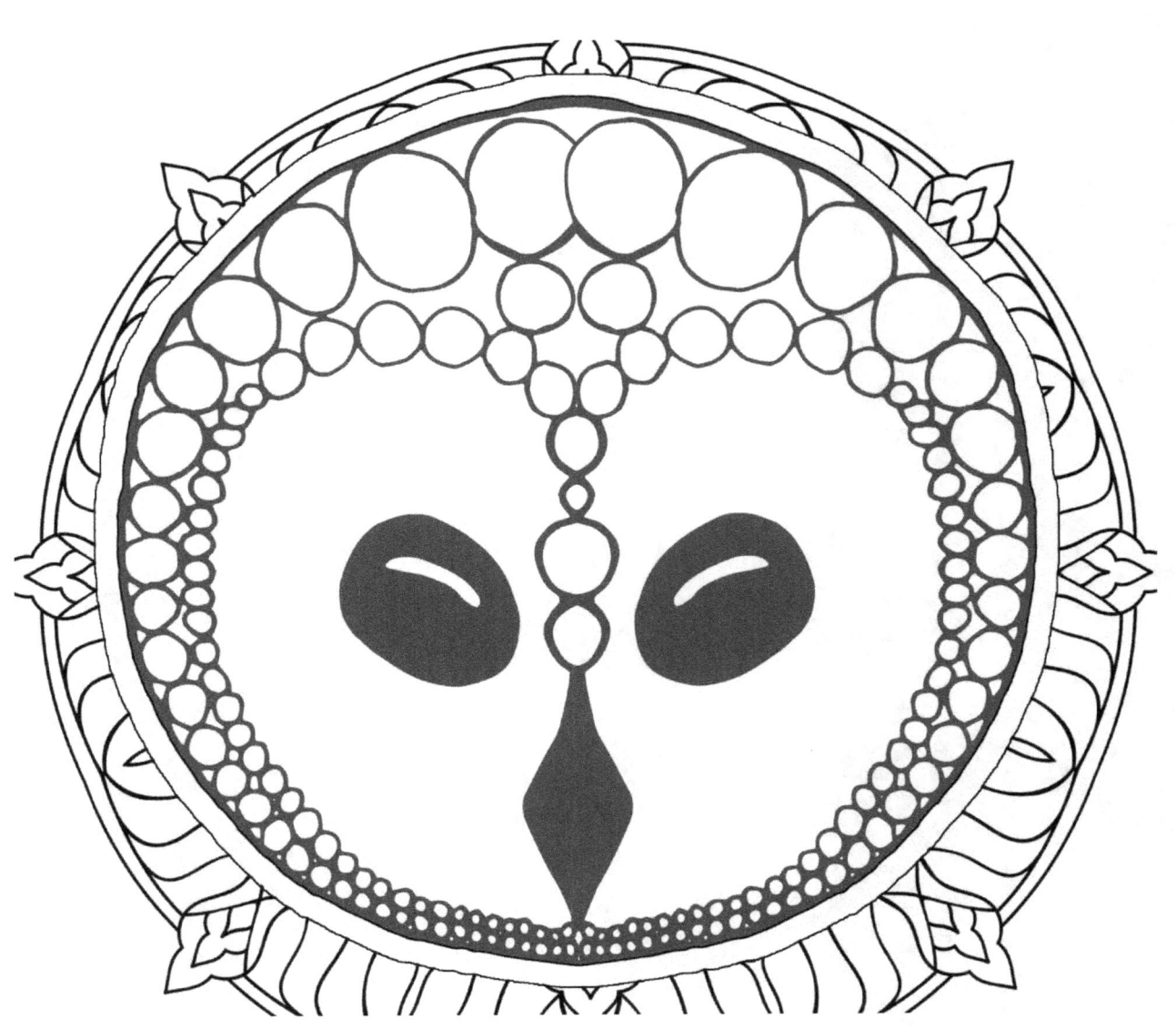

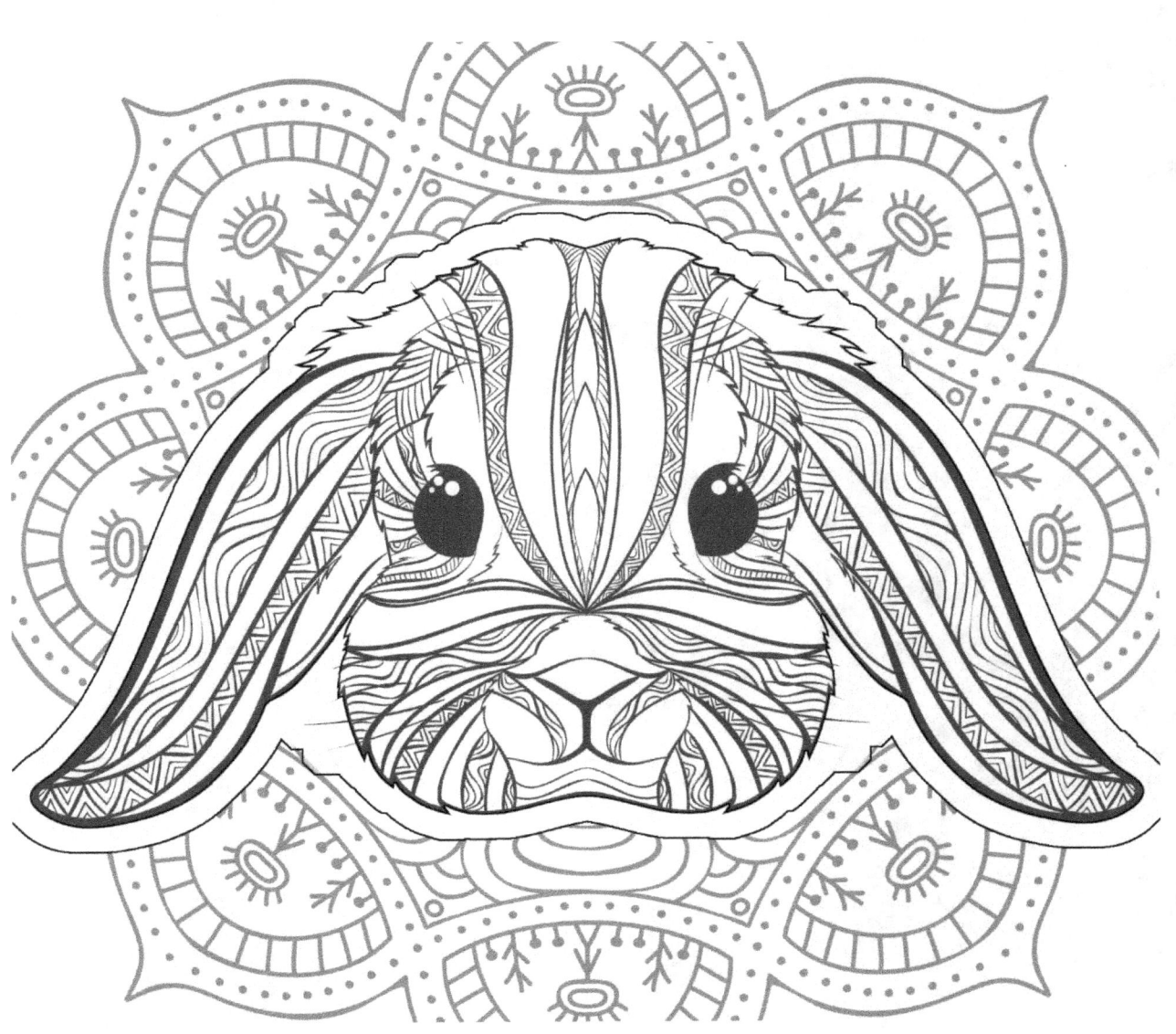

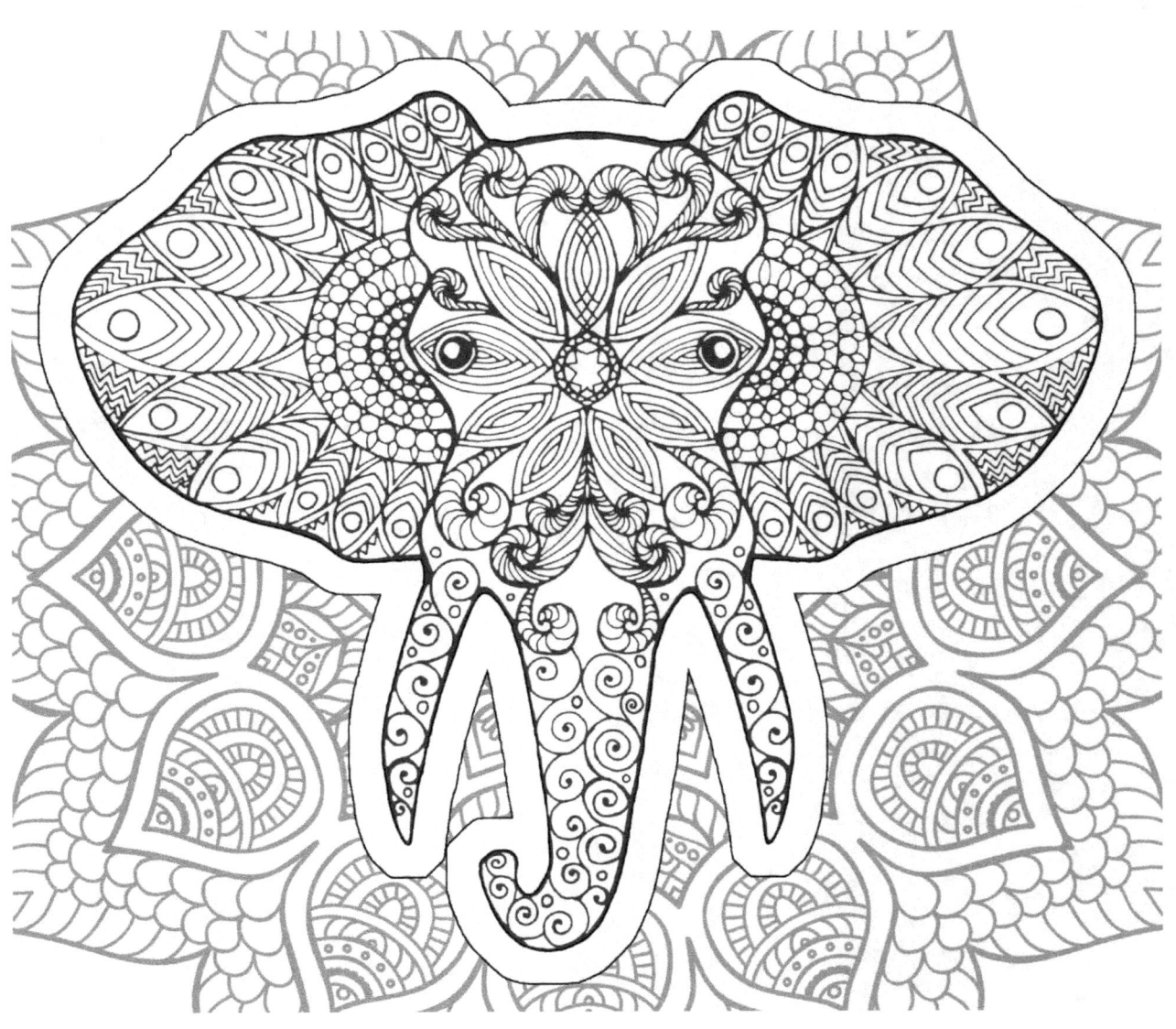

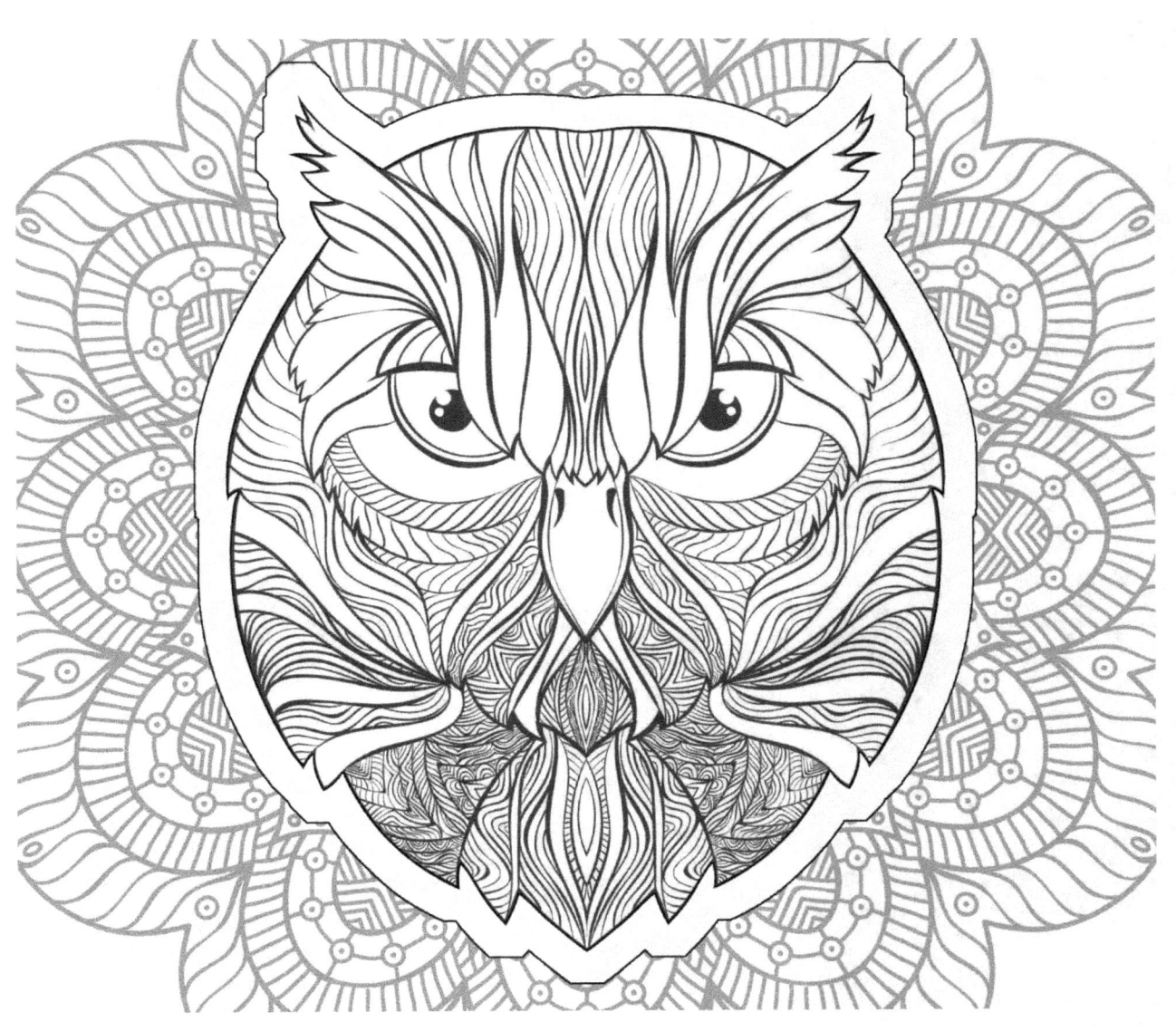

PDF Version this book : http://bit.ly/animals_p_m_1

Don't Miss Another our Books.

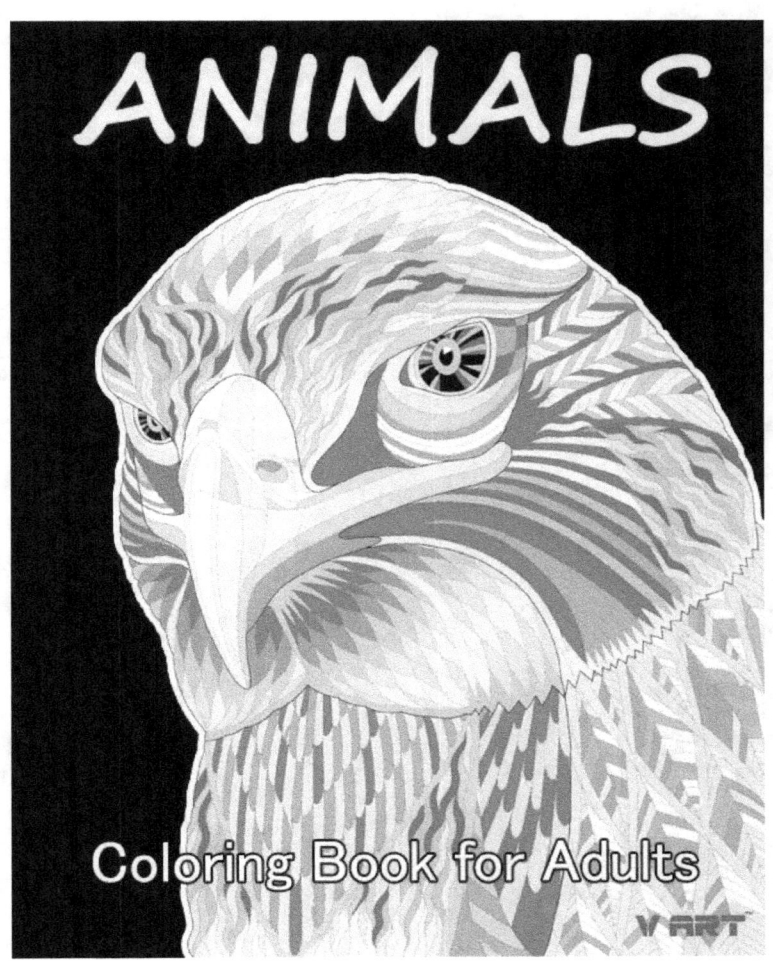

http://bit.ly/safari_coloring_b

ISBN : 9781523987931
(Use this ISBN for searching on amazon.com)